# A COLLECTION OF
# HUMOROUS AND HEART WARMING
# LETTERS TO SANTA

For more information about Santa's
current activities and latest publications,
visit his HomePage on the Internet. The address is
http://www.1earth.com/santa/

## TO MY WIFE JOANNE

And our children, Christopher Charles, Jennifer Lynne, Jennifer Elizabeth, Nichole Marie and our newest addition Rachel Erin, who believe in me and give me the inspiration and love that is so needed in day to day life.

A special thank you to my good friends Steve and Bonnie. Your valuable contributions will never be forgotten.

## A SPECIAL DEDICATION

To every child that comes into this world with only the God given instincts of Love, with a small hand grasping for understanding and warmth, and with a voice crying out for love. They know nothing else until we teach them. May we all be a little kinder to the little voice that comes from below our knees with a question that seems meaningless. For if we don't teach love and understanding, our children will perish at the hands of each other.

## About The Author

Bruce McGuy is a 37 year old contractor. He was born and raised in Fresno, California and moved to the San Jose area upon graduation from high school. He and his wife Joanne are the proud parents of a toddler, as well as having two children each from a previous marriage.

After surviving a troubled childhood, in which Christmas provided some of his best memories, Bruce determined that he would make a difference for other children, especially those who come from troubled homes. Through his seemingly endless energy, creative ability, and tenacious dedication, Bruce has devoted time and resources to fulfilling his personal commitment to children coming from dysfunctional homes. Whether it is his involvement with the local school, coaching Little League, or simply being the neighborhood Santa Claus at Christmas time, Bruce has clearly shown that his love and concern for children is more than just words.

At Christmas time, the decorations on his home make it a community event. Playing Santa Claus each night, Bruce has the opportunity to personally hear the heartfelt wishes of hundreds of boys and girls, many of whom have stories that would break the hearts of the most hardened individuals. From their simple requests for toys to the expression of their deepest inner feelings, Bruce leaves them feeling as though they REALLY have met Santa Claus. As you read their letters, and Santa's responses, see if you can't feel the magic.

# INTRODUCTION

*Even Santa Laughs Sometimes* is a book full of love, written by bright-eyed boys and girls, who have some real questions (and answers) about how the world appears to them. I hope, that after reading this very special Collection of Humorous and Heart Warming Letters to Santa, you will come away with a greater understanding of how children think about their world and what's in it.

*Even Santa Laughs Sometimes* is filled with children's letters which ask questions of and disclose messages to Santa. Every letter in my book was personally presented to me by one of the thousands of children that come to visit my home each year. I make sure each child receives a response to his/her letter whenever possible. My Santa's mailbox overflows during the Christmas season. Even during the summer months I receive postmarked letters to Santa at my home, from children from all over the United States, wanting to know what I am up to. During the Christmas season I welcome over 20,000 visitors to my home to share in the Christmas spirit.

I want to take this opportunity to thank all of you for making my first book *Even Santa Cries Sometimes* a tremendous success. From the hundreds of letters I've received about my first book, I have read how much my book has changed your lives for the better. This has truly made me feel that I have received the most special gift of my life. Thank you very much.

# "EVEN SANTA LAUGHS SOMETIMES"

I thought I might share one of my most memorable recollections of being Santa Claus. It came upon an unusually cold December night. I was in the process of repairing some of my outside Christmas lights when children with their parents started to gather for the upcoming visit of Santa Claus. While they waited, parents were busy buttoning up their children's coats and helping them go over their lists, making sure they hadn't forgotten anything important.

I recognized many of the children and their parents from years past. It seemed odd though, I knew who they were and yet they hadn't recognized me without my Santa suit. As I continued working on my lights, I started to listen to what each child was reciting from their Christmas list. It was as if I was invisible, walking among them, hearing every word they said. As the time neared for Santa's visit, I quietly slipped away and started dressing, all the while remembering what I had overheard.

I entered the front yard with bells a-jingling and laughing my special Santa laugh. The children's eyes quickly lit up with anticipation. It was all their parents could do to hold them back until I was in place for them. Doris was the first to come and give me a hug. As I knelt down on one knee, arms open, she started telling me a story of her pet hamster and how her pet had been very sick, but seems to be well now. She then explained to me what her pet hamster wanted for Christmas and proceeded to give me the hamster's Christmas list. I took the opportunity to tell Doris what Rudolph and I thought she might want for Christmas. You should have seen her mouth drop open, almost as wide as her eyes. All she could do was stare at me with a puzzled look. I gave Doris another hug and we said our goodbyes.

Next in line was Ken Jr., age 8, and his sister, Sara, age 5. After our hugs and conversations about school and what's going on in their world, we got down to Santa's list. All it took was Ken Jr. asking me if I knew what he wanted for Christmas, and before he could utter another syllable I began to tell him and Sara what I thought they might like for presents. Ken and Sara were both delighted when they heard that they would receive just what they wanted. With their letters to Santa still in hand, they proceeded to run back to their father Ken., Sr.

Ken Sr. handed me his children's letters along with a handshake and a look of bewilderment. His eyes searched deep into mine, as if he was looking for an explanation as to what just happened. I saw a spark of life come to his eyes and with that Ken Sr. asked "What do I want for Christmas Santa."

I thought, "Testing me is he?" I looked to his wife, then back to Ken Sr. I replied, "Yes I do know what you want, but you won't be receiving it in time for this Christmas. You'll both receive your gift in late June or early July of next year."

With that, Ken turned to his wife and she nodded, yes. I could tell at that moment I was wrong, Ken actually did receive the gift he wanted for this Christmas. With tears in their eyes they said goodbye and headed for home.

You might be wondering, how did I know? I don't know, I don't have all the answers. I'm only Santa Claus.

Wishing you a very Merry Christmas.

Love, Santa

Dear Santa,

Last year you brought me a telephone. I want to thank you. For Christmas this year, enclosed you will find my phone bill from last year. Since you brought me the phone, Dad said you should get the bills.

Thanks,

Marie

*Dear Marie,*

*Please leave the phone next to the fireplace Christmas Eve.*

*Thanks,*
*Santa*

Dear Santa,

My name is Susan and I am three years old. I am finally excited about Christmas. For Christmas I want a Playskool doll house, a tricycle, dishes, a doll with a bottle, but not one for me. I am a big girl now. Also I want blocks and a toy stocking.

I don't know what you would like better, so I'm going to leave out zucchini loaf and banana chip cookies for you, but could you leave one bite for me? We're coming to see you tonight, but Randy is not coming. He was very naughty. He played with Daddy's battery operated drill and drilled a few hundred holes in his bedroom door. He's going to come another Christmas, maybe!

I love you, Santa. I've been good. Please bring me what I said, and please don't forget Randy.

Thank you very much,

    Susan

*Dear Susan,*

*Tell Daddy not to be too hard on Randy for I remember Daddy telling me a story about when he himself took his daddy's hammer and fixed the front of his mommy's car real good. Tell Dad I'll bring some wood putty for him. I'll bet it was Mommy's idea to leave some of those wonderful treats. I'll make sure I also leave Mommy some bites too.*

*See you real soon.*

    *Love,*

        *Santa*

**Dear Santa Claus,**

**If I tell you a lie you won't bring me any presents. Why?**

**Jamie**

*Dear Jamie,*

*Santa has never told you that he wouldn't bring you any presents if you ever told a lie. Sometimes parents tell stories about children that don't receive any presents from Santa if they've lied. Although I have never told you such a thing, I want you to know it could happen if you lie too much. Its best not to take the chance. One lie too many could cost you a Christmas. Be good.*

*Love,*
*Santa*

Dear Santa,

When we take Fred for a walk we take along a pooper scooper with us. What do you bring with you on Christmas Eve?

Love,

Lynn, James, Fred, Doris, and dog Fredie

*Dear Lynn,*

*What does Santa take along Christmas Eve? That all depends. But first I have a question for you. Do you take Fred, your dad, for a walk, or is it Fredie the dog you're referring to as Fred? Please let me know for my records, and if it is Fred, your dad, what kind of collar would he like for Christmas?*

*Anyway, to answer your question, I don't take anything along. I make sure that the reindeer don't eat for 36 hours before flight, so we don't have any problems or law suits.*

*Thanks for asking,*

*Love,*
*Santa*

Dear Santa,

I am twelve years old and am writing this letter for my little brother Donald who will be 6 years old on December 25th. Donald loves to go camping more than anything else. It never snows here at home so Donald would like you to bring him a sleigh full of white snow to play in. Donald wants to sleep outside and have you drop it on him so when he wakes up he will be covered in the cold, white snow. Also please bring Donald a remote control car, Barney toys, a soccer ball, and don't forget the snow!

Love,

Cathy and Donald

P.S. Donald wants me to remind you not to throw the toys out with the snow.

*Dear Cathy and Donald,*

*The fact that you, Cathy, took the time to write to Santa for your little brother tells me there is great bond between the two of you that will allow both of you to be able to depend on each other later in life. I can't bring you any gift greater than the one you already share with each other. But, I can bring you most of what you asked for. Except the snow. Yes, there is plenty of snow here at the North Pole, except by the time I get to your house it will be rain. I don't want Donald to get wet on his birthday.*

*Love,*

*Santa*

Dear Santa,

Sorry about the big stocking! How are you? I'm fine. How many elves do you have? Who's your favorite elf? How's Mrs. Claus? I wonder if I'll become like you someday? I can't wait until Christmas. All I want for Christmas is a BB gun, (I won't shoot anyone), a Super Duper Double Looper, Sparking Hot Rods, a VCR, and my mom and dad to get back together. (live together I mean)

Well, bye,
Marty, 12 years old


*Dear Marty,*

*If your stocking is as large as last year, I'm sure it probably will be an extra trip again this year. Thanks for the prior warning.*

*Marty, Santa is not perfect, but I do my best to love everyone, to care about them and their problems, and to give of myself. I believe you too can be just like me. It's not easy. Most people talk about all the great things they're going to do to help those in need and yet those are only words. I know you are going through some very difficult times in your life. Right now, your letter shows me you're reaching out to find someone or something to show you the way. If you show love to all who are around you most of the time, you will stand out from the crowd and be recognized by those people such as Santa. They will be neighbors, friends, or family and will be there to help you along the way.*

*Don't forget to write next year. I want to know how things are going.*

*Love,*
*Santa*

Dear Santa,

What is brown and red and goes round and round?

Answer: Rudolph in a blender

Ha! Ha! Ha!

Randy, age 9

*Dear John K.*

*I know your real name isn't Randy, and I know your name is John. Rudolph thought your joke was pretty funny. Rudolph has a joke for you. What is nine years old and cries on Christmas morning? A little boy named John. Ha! Ha! Ha!*

*Love,*

*Santa & Rudolph*

*(Although John signed his name Randy, John's mom wrote John's name and address on the upper left corner of the envelope before mailing it. That's how Santa knew.)*

Dear Santa,

Hi, my name is Josh and I want $10.00 for something I want to buy from my friend. I live at 999 California. Please try to get it for me, I have been very good this year.

Love,

Josh

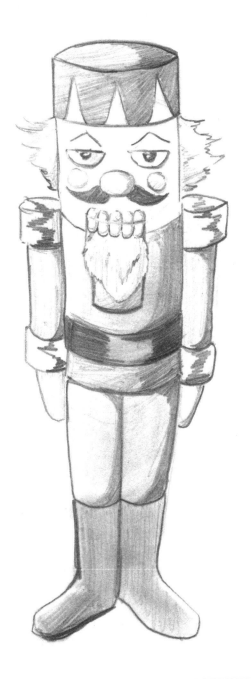

Dear Josh,

I can tell by your letter that you can't wait for Christmas so enclosed you will find the new $10.00 bill that you asked for. Please tell your mom where you got it so she knows.

See you soon,

Love,

Santa

Dear Santa,

1. A baby brother in March
2. My baby brother or sister to be healthy
3. A stuffed animal for my baby brother because he will miss Christmas
4. A remote for my TV
5. Some paper clips
6. I want more than 9 presents, but can't think of them.

Angel, age 10

*Dear Angel,*

*Santa can already tell what a wonderful big sister you will be for your new baby brother or sister. I will try to bring you those special 9 presents you've forgotten about. Rudolph will pack something special just for you.*

*Love,*

*Santa*

Dear Santa,

What I want for Christmas is a picture of my grandma. She died and I want to make sure she's OK in Heaven.

And a robot to do my chores for me.

Thanks,
Kimberly

*Dear Kimberly,*

*Santa's grandma is in Heaven too. I miss her very much. I think about her from time to time and of all the wonderful things we did together. I love my grandma even though she is in Heaven and I can't see her or hug her any more. She is in my heart just the same way your grandma is in your heart and memory.*

*I am sorry I can't get a picture of your grandma for you. Tonight, before I go to sleep, I will ask my grandma up in Heaven to watch after your grandma for you.*

*Love always,*
*Santa*

Dear Santa,

    All I want is money and I want it now . . .

        Thanks,

        Kim

P.S.    S.A.S.E. enclosed, no checks please.

*Dear Kim,*

    *Many children and adults don't really know what they want for Christmas. I am so happy you don't have that problem so I would like to give you what you asked for. Except you forgot to tell me how much money you needed. I guess you really didn't know what you wanted after all.*

*Looking forward to your next letter.*

    *Love,*

        *Santa*

Dear Santa,

Last year you didn't bring me any money. I forgot to tell you how much I needed. Ten million will do.

Thanks,
Kim

P.S.    S.A.S.E. enclosed, no checks please.

Dear Kim,

*Thank you for your letter again this year. I see once again you're asking for cold hard cash. I would like to give you what you've asked for except you didn't tell me what kind of money you wanted, peso, franc, U.S. currency, etc. Where do you plan to spend your money? What do you want to buy? Let me know next year.*

*Love,*

*Santa*

Dear Santa,

OK, lets get is right this time. Its been three years and still no cash. I am fourteen years old now and almost ready to start collecting Social Security. So hurry up and bring me my damn money before the government starts taxing me on it. Now, I need one million from 2 years ago, 10 million from last year and 20 million for this year. All U.S. cash money! I'll even change my policy and accept checks with the proper ID.

Love,

Kim

P.S.     S.A.S.E. enclosed, C.O.D. accepted.

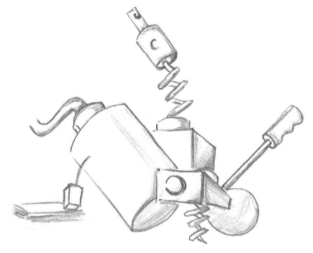

*Dear Kim,*

*I have some very bad news for you. I am sorry to say in July of this year Santa's printing press blew up. At this time I can't even print any money to help repair it. If only you really knew what you had wanted in the years past. It just goes to show you just when you think you've got a sure thing, things can go wrong. Don't be discouraged. Before long you will be getting a job that pays you money and you won't be asking Santa for any.*

*Love,*

*Santa*

Dear Santa,

Thank you for all your letters. It was a lot of fun sharing them with my friends. We got a lot of laughs from them. I'll still take the cash owed from previous years if you ever get the printing press going again. This year please bring me a new boy friend that is cute and a nice guy.

That's all.

Thanks,

Kim

P.S.    S.A.S.E. Box enclosed to mail him in, No dummies please.

Dear Kim,

It has been a wonderful experience for me writing to you over the last few years. I hope you will continue to write and tell me how things are going with you.

By the way, its against the law to mail cute, nice boys in boxes.

See you soon,

Santa

Dear Santa,

How are you? Is it cold where you live?

Please bring me:

1. The Barbie family
2. Little Miss Magic Jewels
3. A large doll
4. A teddy bear

We will have a fire in our chimney so please be very careful when you come to our house. Just in case, Mommy will leave a medical supply box next to the fireplace (next to the cookies and milk).

Thank you Santa,

Betty

P.S. I am 5 years old.

*Dear Betty,*

*In answer to your letter, Santa Claus is just fine. I feel like I am under 100 years old, and yes, its very cold here at the North Pole. I'll be very careful of the fire in your fireplace. I wouldn't want your presents to get burned, or Santa, for that matter. Thank you for letting me know, and I won't forget your presents. Remind Mommy and Daddy to check the batteries in your smoke detector, OK?*

*Love,*
*Santa*

Dear Santa,

For Christmas this year I would like for my best friend, Ann, to come visit me. Ann moved last year so please stop by her house at 1413 Miller Ave. Pick her up for me and bring her to my house. You don't need to wrap her up or anything like that, just make sure she is dressed so she won't get too cold on the trip.

Thanks,

Your friend, Venice

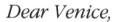

Dear Venice,

*Each year you seem to out do yourself. In all my years, I can't remember anyone ever having such unusual requests. Last year you wanted me to pick up some pizza on the way. As long as I was going by, why not, you said. This year you want a friend delivered. I don't do pick-ups or deliveries, that includes friends, family, pizzas or take out burgers.*

*Can't wait till next year.*

*Love,*

*Santa*

Dear Santa,

What is big and red and flies in the air?

The big red toy you brought me. It wasn't the one I wanted. Next time only bring me what I ordered.

Sincerely.

Joey

*Dear Joey,*

*After receiving your letter I was at a loss for words. I decided that if that's how you appreciate the toys you receive, then maybe next year I'll give your toys to someone who will appreciate being given a present. If you really don't want the toy ask Mom to give it to one of the abused and battered women's shelters for the children that are temporarily living away from their homes and may not have had a toy for Christmas at all.*

*Love,*

*Santa*

Dear Santa Claus,

The Santa at the mall told me he is the REAL Santa Claus. When I pulled his hair, it came off. Don't bring him any presents, he told me a lie.

John


*Dear John,*

*Thank you for your letter to Santa. It was a joy to read. I don't believe the Santa at the mall meant to lie to you. I think he was just trying to help you to believe in Santa Claus. And John, if I don't bring him presents then what would happen if you told a little lie to someone? I wouldn't be able to bring you a present either, would I? Santa loves everyone. I don't choose those that I love by their behavior as much as for the love in their hearts.*

*All my love,*
*Santa*

Dear Santa,

Mommy says that Mrs. Claus puts you on a diet after Christmas, just like my daddy. How come you eat so much?

Liz,

*Dear Liz,*

*Mommy is right! Mrs. Claus does put me on a diet after Christmas. Sometimes, when Mrs. Claus isn't watching, I sneak out to visit Rudolph, and he shares some of his carrot ice cream with me.*

*Why do I eat so much? I wish I knew!*

*See you soon,*

*Santa*

Dear Santa Claus,

    I hope you have a good Christmas! Tell Mrs. Claus I said hi. I know that Christmas is for sharing and being nice to everyone. I will try my best to be nice all year long. I want two roller blades. But maybe you can bring me one of them and give the other to a homeless kid. And maybe if I ask all my friends to do the same then all the homeless kids will have a Christmas.

Sincerely,

        Michele

(no return address)

Dear Santa,

Knock Knock
Who's there?
Santa Claus
Santa Claus who?
Santa Claus and Rudolph
with my presents:
A train set, a remote
control truck, a car, a
bike, a bird cage, a yellow
bird, bird food, a color
TV, a room to myself, a
radio, clothes

       Love,
         Dave

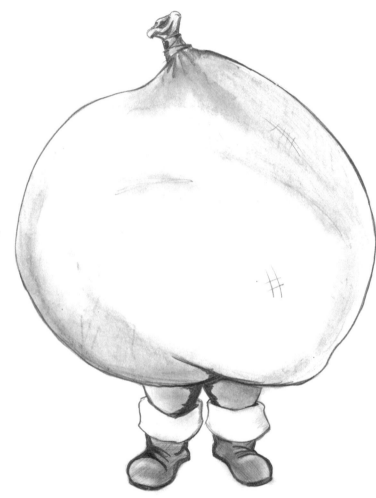

*Dear Dave,*

*Knock Knock*
*Who's there?*
*Santa Claus*
*Santa Claus who?*
*Santa Claus and Rudolph*
*with a bag so full of your*
*presents we have to use*
*the front door.*

       *Love,*
        *Santa*

Dear Santa,

My uncle says you're not a very nice person and that you work your elves all day and all night long and don't pay them any money. That's not very nice. What I would like for Christmas is Barbies, a color TV, a VCR, a radio, shoes, a dress, pants (5 colored pair), rings, bracelets, socks, a watch, nail polish, new carpet for my bedroom (pink with a little yellow), a new phone, and a computer system.

Sam

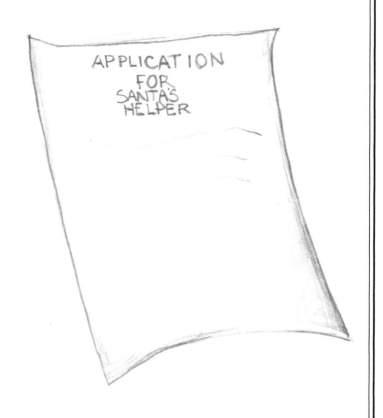

APPLICATION FOR SANTA'S HELPER

*Dear Sam,*

*I just want you to know that the elves love what they do and can leave any time they would like to. They work 3 months out of each year and relax for 9 months. They eat for free, travel all over the world by way of the sleigh and have unlimited insurance coverage. They live in 3000 square foot homes, with heated pools and spas, free phones, toys, games, hair cuts, etc. If you believe they work too hard then maybe next year you should cut your list in half and they can relax. As for your uncle, I think he needs to get a life, and let him know I'm not accepting any applications at this time.*

*Santa*

Dear Santa,

My daddy told me that your sleigh put holes in our roof. He told me he is going to write to you for money to fix it. I don't think you did it. Next year could you bring Daddy a new house? It doesn't have to be too big, maybe just 500,000 feet or so.

Ronda

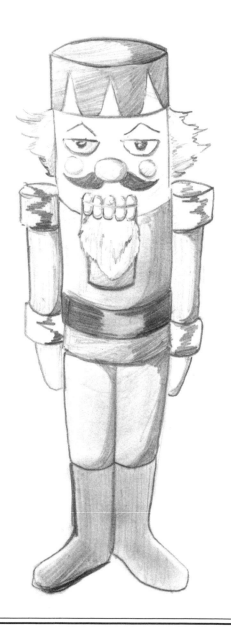

*Dear Ronda,*

*So far I haven't received a letter or a repair bill from your dad. Tell Dad that I do remember your roof because it made it very difficult to land. The bright lights from inside your house beamed through the roof, temporarily blinding Rudolph, and we almost crashed. If it wasn't for Rudolph's quick maneuvering, it would have been a very messy situation. (Reindeer stew time).*

*See you next year,*

*Santa*

Dear Santa Claus,

I already wrote a letter to Santa Claus but I'm just saying Merry Christmas. I love you.

Love,

Jennifer G.

*Dear Jennifer G.*

*Merry Christmas. I love you too.*

*Love,*

*Santa*

Dear Santa,

Could you tell me a little bit about your house at the North Pole? Also, please bring me a new bike, roller blades, and extra clothes.

Stan

*Dear Stan,*

*Santa's house is a wonderful place. We have many bedrooms, plenty of bathrooms, and one large fireplace where Santa hangs his pants to dry. Mrs. Claus is a wonderful cook and we enjoy all the company that visits.*

*The most special thing about Santa's house is the love we feel for everyone that comes to visit. Santa's house is filled to the brim with love. I like to feel my home is a special place, but I know there are many homes such as ours. Whether small studio apartments or large mansions, love has a way of filling the rooms with a special feeling that makes all homes as special as Santa's.*

*And I won't forget your presents.*

*Love,*

*Santa*

Dear Santa Claus,

This is what I want for Christmas. I would like for my grandpa to stop telling me stupid bedtime stories. Please bring him X-MEN comic books to read to me, roller blades for Dad (size 12), roller blades for me (size 7), pads, helmets, and a new play toy for my little sister.

Thanks,

Tim, age 10

*Dear Tim,*

*I think it's wonderful that you enjoy letting grandpa tell you bedtime stories, and for you to ask for more stories for Grandpa. I receive so many letters from children wishing their grandpas were still alive because they miss them so. It's great to find a young man as yourself helping your grandpa stay up with the times. I'm sure I'll be able to find plenty of X-MEN comics for the two of you to share.*

*Love,*

*Santa Claus*

To Santa Claus,

I've been a good boy.
I obey my Mom and Dad.
I want a gun,
A GI Joe,
Stunt cycle,
X-MEN,
Hockey sticks, and
Boxing gloves.

   Love,

      Nick

*Dear Nick,*

*You have quite a little list this year. I see you want a gun. I'm sure a play toy gun is what you wanted, however, I'm not sure we have any. I'll check, and if we do I'll double check with your mother to be sure it's okay to bring you one. I am sure we have most of the other toys you have asked for.*

*See you soon,*
   *Love,*
      *Santa*

Dear Santa,

A new dog
A new cat
Two rabbits
One *very* small cow
Two sheep
A baby brother to play with
And four new toys

That's all.

Love,

Randy

(no return address)

Dear Santa,

My aunt wants me to ask you how you stay so thin? She wants to know what Mrs. Claus cooks for you. My Aunt May has lost 178 pounds so far. How much have you lost?

Love,

Phyllis

Dear Phyllis,

*Mrs. Claus makes sure Santa doesn't get too big for his britches, that is for sure. Mrs. Claus is a wonderful cook! Even Rudolph enjoys her stews (as long as they are not reindeer). Santa really hasn't lost any weight. I stay pretty much the same except for Christmas time, when I eat so many cookies and drink too much milk.*

*I want you to tell Aunt May that Santa is very proud of her for what she has been doing. I can't begin to imagine how difficult it must be, but my heart and love go out to her and to you, Phyllis.*

*Love,*

*Santa*

Dear Santa,

Ralph is only 5 years old and has asked me to write this letter for him.

For Grandma, please bring a new monster truck, (a real one).

Grandpa would like a play hammer so he won't hurt himself anymore.

For Uncle David, a new watch that works so he will stop getting fired for being late to work.

For big sis, a new bottle of perfume that smells good, I used hers all up.

And for Jack, a new dog bone. One *so big* he can't bury it.

And for Mom and Dad a few toys.

As for myself, a new play house, before Grandpa looses a finger building me one.

Love,
Ralph and Mommy

P.S.   We came to your house on December 23rd. What a wonderful thing you do for all of us.

Thank you

(no return address)

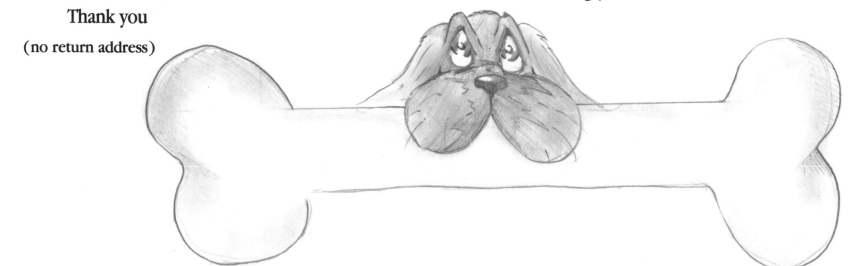

Dear Santa Claus,

My friend told me you laugh all the time. Don't you get the hiccups?

Love,

Brian

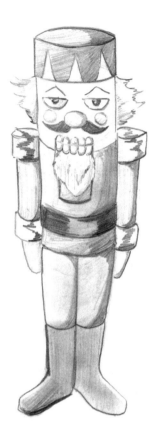

Dear Brian,

Santa is a jolly old soul and enjoys laughing as much as possible. Only once in a while do I get the hiccups. Usually its Mrs. Claus who gets them, from laughing at Santa.

Love,

Santa

Dear Santa Claus,

I love you and want to know if you and Mrs. Claus ever get a divorce will you call my mom? She needs someone that's nice like you.

Love,

Nicole R.

*Dear Nicole,*

*Thank you for thinking of Santa. With such a wonderful daughter watching out for her, I'm sure your mom will find just the right person to share her life with.*

*Love always,*

*Santa*

Dear Santa,

My name is Ben, and I am 5 years old. This is what I would like for Christmas this year. Mommy says I've been good so you can bring everything I ask for, so here is my list.

A Dizzy Dinosaur
Play Dough
Power Rangers, the good guys only
NO BAD GUYS
Small bike
Toy train
and Mommy says you need to spend some of my toy money
on new clothes for me.

Love you Santa,
From Ben

P.S.   Mom wrote this letter for Ben, but they were Ben's words.

*Dear Ben,*

*I was glad to hear how good you have been again this year. I am sure you didn't want a real dizzy dinosaur so I'll bring you a Dizzy Dinosaur toy, and no BAD GUYS.*

*See you soon.*
*Love,*
*Santa*

Dear Santa,

    I just want to love you.

Rachel R.

This isn't a "Dear Santa" letter. It's a "Thank you" letter. It's easy to lose the Christmas spirit amidst the hustle-bustle of finding the best present, the traffic, and the bitchy customers ( I work in retail). Somehow the joy and love of the season get tarnished by the materialistic aspects of the holidays.

One night after work, I thought I had become tarnished myself. I stopped by your house on the way home. I sat for a long while, awestruck by the beautiful lights.

I don't know what happened, but it all came back to me. Not like when I was a kid getting up at 6:30 in the morning to see what Santa left in the stockings, or if he ate all the cookies. I realized it's a time of love and sharing. A time to say or do for people we care about that maybe we didn't do enough for before. And though things in my life seem like they couldn't be worse, I've learned that there will *always* be *something* to brighten your day . . . it's just sometimes you have to look for it!

Thanks for lighting up my day and my Christmas Spirit!

Happy Holidays to You All!!

Dear Santa,

I don't know if you'll receive this letter before Christmas, but I wanted to tell you that I already received my gift from you this Christmas.

I am 25 years old, and six years ago this month I was blessed with my son Vincent (Vinnie). Vinnie is a miracle child in my eyes. I was told when he was born that he might not live more than a few days. He had several complications and could not breathe on his own. At 4 days old the doctors performed a tracheotomy on him, and he remained in the hospital until he was ten months old. The trach was removed right before his third birthday. It was one of the happiest days of my life. Besides a few minor surgeries that he still has to go through, he is a healthy child with a lot of life to share.

The gift you have given to me is the chance for my son and I to come to your home. I have always believed in the spirit of Santa, and after having a child it all comes back to you. It was truly an amazing experience for my son and me.

I thank you for giving me this pleasure, just when things could be better in my life. After reading your book, *Even Santa Cries Sometimes*, I realized that things could always be worse. You, yourself, are amazing. I love you. May all your dreams come true for you and your family all year around.

Love,

Nicole,
The Believer

Dear Santa Claus - AKA Bruce McGuy,

How special a person you are to me. Of all my childhood memories, you are what I remember most. I can still remember the cold December nights when I was a little girl waiting in line at your home to visit with you.

What I remember most are your large hands extended, to openly await my arrival, and the warmth of your hugs and kisses. Your low, soothing voice spoke words of love and had a kind of gentleness. You made me feel so special when I was in your arms. Now in some little way I hope to return something to you. I want you to know how special you made me feel, and how I learned by your example, that it is better to give than to receive. To share a gift of love is better than all things. No one knows that better than you.

As I see Santas all over the malls and in the stores, I think of you. I know you don't do what you do for money, for you ask nothing in return. You never judge or criticize. You love all children never minding their race. There is something very special about you that sets you apart from all the Santas of the world. You are, and always will be, *Santa Claus* to me. I pray for you always. I think how blessed the children are that have been held in your arms. Children can feel the difference between you, the *real Santa Claus,* and those who are substitutes. I am one of the fortunate ones that can say "I have loved and hugged the real Santa Claus and he has loved and held me."

P.S. I just finished your first book, *Even Santa Cries Sometimes*. Never in my life have I been so immensely wrapped up in a book. It is the best book I have ever read and I will be sharing it with my friends and family. And once again, the fact that you return the profits back to the children, strengthens my belief in who you are.

Love,
 Carol K.

*I would like to share with you a few Christmas stories written by children. I think you will enjoy them.*

## THE LIVING TREE

It was a cold night in Treeville. My friends and I lived on a small hill. We were pine trees. We were grown to be used as Christmas decorations.

"I can't wait to be cut down for Christmas," I said.

"Neither can I," said another tree.

A little while later headlights came up from around the hill. Men came out from a big white truck with tools. The next thing my friend and I knew, we were laying on the ground and then being piled into a truck. We were driven to the Treeville's Christmas tree patch. A little while later, we were standing up in bowls of water, with lots of other trees surrounding us. Many people came by, looking up and down my leaves, only to leave and look at another tree. Pretty soon almost every tree on the lot was gone, but I was still there.

Then a little boy and girl came up to me and yelled "Mommy, Daddy, we like this one."

So they took me home and put jewels on me and a pretty silver angel on the top of me. They put a little train that moved under me.

For the next couple of days I watched my new family. They were running around putting decorations on the walls and in the windows. They put big red and white socks over the fire in the fireplace. The mommy and daddy put presents into the big socks. One night they put a few presents under me. They had friends and family come over and had a party. Little kids came and looked at me and talked about some guy named Santa. After everyone went home, my family went to bed.

A little while later a big man came down the chimney. He had a long white beard and white hair, rosy cheeks, and a cherry nose. He was wearing a red velvet outfit and hat, black boots, and a black belt. He seemed very happy as he immediately went to work. He started putting presents in the red and white stockings over the fireplace. Then he came over and put presents under me.

When he finished he went over to the plate of cookies and ate all but one bite and then drank the milk the children had left out for him. He took the carrots they had left and put them in his bag for the reindeer. He then walked over to me, looked at me, touched my decorations and felt my branches. His hands and fingers were soft and plump. He then walked over to the fireplace, turned around and took one last look at the room, then drifted up the chimney.

The next morning, my family woke me up by running into the room and grabbing presents from their stockings and out from under me.

The children were happy, saying "Mommy, Daddy, look what I got."

"That's nice," they would say, smiling to each other.

I'm happy my family was happy and that I brought some of their joy to them.

The End

Jenny M. & Lauren J.

# THE DAY CHILDREN SAVED CHRISTMAS

It was a cold winter's morning and I was on my way outside to get the newspaper for my mom. As I bent over to get the newspaper, I saw a red and green flier stapled to the newspaper bag. Fliers don't really interest my family or me, so I ripped it off, crinkled it up, and threw it on the ground. When I got to the front door of our house, I noticed taped to the door was the same red and green flier. I thought maybe I should read it. This is what it said:

Santa is looking for responsible children to help him make toys for children all around the world. Santa's elves have caught a serious cold, and without help, there may be no Christmas.

I don't believe in Santa, so once again I crinkled the flier up and threw it on the ground. When I got into the house, my mom had made a huge breakfast. Things like eggs, bacon, toast, ham and hash browns were on our table.

"Janice, is there anything special you would like for Christmas from Santa?" Dad asked.

"Dad, you know I don't believe in Santa, that's just a bunch of hocus pocus," Janice exclaimed.

"Janice," my mother scolded, "don't talk like that! Why don't you go clean your room or something?"

"But Mom," I moaned.

"No buts, Janice, now go do what you were told," mom said.

So I went to my room. When I opened my door, I felt some kind of power surge through my body. It made me feel kind of strange, so I decided to climb into bed. I got into bed and tried to go to sleep.

"Ow . . . get off me," something mumbled from underneath my pillow.

"What, who said that?" I asked in shock.

"I did," said this two inch elf, who came crawling out from underneath my pillow.

"Who are you?" I asked

"I'm Elfy, and I came to take you back to the North Pole with me," he said.

"You did, did you? Well, I have news for you mister, I'm not going to the North Pole with you because I don't believe in Santa," I snarled.

"I know," said Elfy.

"You do, how?" I asked.

"Easy, every Christmas you ask for one thing."

"What's that?"

"Nothing." I just sat there looking at Elfy like he was crazy. "Anyway, the reason I came here is because Santa needs help," he insisted.

"This is not happening, this is all just a nightmare," Janice insisted, "I know I shouldn't have read that stupid flier in the mail, now I'm dreaming about it. Great!"

"This isn't a nightmare, this isn't even a dream. It's real, now come with me," Elfy said.

"I'm not coming with you, I don't even believe in Santa, so why do you have to pick me?" I complained.

"Why do you have to make things so complicated?" Elfy said moaning. "Santa wants me to gather all of the non-believers to take to his workshop to show them that there is a Santa, and to make Christmas a better time."

"Oh, fine, I'll go with you, but can we make it quick? I have to be home before dinner," I finally agreed.

We went to the North Pole in the blink of an eye. "Come," said Elfy. "We have a lot of work to accomplish." Two hours later we were finished making boats, dolls, trains and every type of toy a kid could dream of.

When Christmas Eve night finally arrived, Santa, Elfy and I set up the sleigh. When the sleigh and reindeer were ready we hopped into the sleigh and Santa screamed, "Now Dasher! Now Dancer! Now Prancer and Vixen! On Comet! On Cupid! On Donder and Blitzen!"

Then off we went, delivering toys everywhere. When we got to my house Santa said goodbye, and he thanked me. Then I knew Santa Claus was real. Do you know what? I think next year I will ask for that horse that I've been wanting.

Bye,

Janice P.
Madera, CA

*Wishing you a very*
*Merry Christmas*

*Santa*

# To Order Additional Copies

## of

## EVEN SANTA LAUGHS SOMETIMES

## or

## EVEN SANTA CRIES SOMETIMES

*Fill out order form and mail to:*

*(Photocopies of Order Form Accepted)*

Home Run Publishing Co.
1083 Golden Acre Court
San Jose, California 95136

•

*Makes A Wonderful Gift*
*For Family And Friends*

Please send me

_____ copies of *Even Santa Laughs Sometimes*
at $7.95 each_____

_____copies of *Even Santa Cries Sometimes*
at $7.95 each_____

Subtotal $_____

CA residents add .65 per copy sales tax

Sales Tax _____
+ 2.00 per copy shipping and handling in U.S.A.
Canada add 4.00 per copy shipping and handling

Total $_____

*Make check or money order in U.S. currency payable to:*

Home Run Publishing Co.
1083 Golden Acre Court
San Jose, California 95136

*Mail to:*

Name _____

Address_____

City _____

State _____ Zip_____

Allow 7 to 10 days for delivery

## ABOUT THE ARTIST

Jeremy Postlewait is an aspiring young artist who demonstrates technical skills and a grasp of the medium that is beyond his years. A California native, Jeremy was born in Alameda and now resides in Madera, where at only 20 years of age he is pursuing a promising career in the arts.

Attending Fresno City College following graduation from Fresno High, Jeremy has already produced a variety of works including numerous cartoons, many highly praised illustrations, and examples of modern comic book art. His artistic contributions to *Even Santa Laughs Sometimes* brings added life and meaning to this special collection of letters to Santa.